Drawing and Learning About Dogs

Using Shapes and Lines

by
Amy Bailey Muehlenhardt

Thanks to our advisers for their expertise, research, and advice:

Cathy Sinning, D.V.M.
Minneapolis, Minnesota

Susan Kesselring, M.A., Literacy Educator
Rosemount-Apple Valley-Eagan (Minnesota) School District

PICTURE WINDOW BOOKS
Minneapolis, Minnesota

Amy Bailey Muehlenhardt
grew up in Fergus Falls, Minnesota,
and attended Minnesota State
University in Moorhead. She holds
a Bachelor of Science degree in
Graphic Design and Art Education.
Before coming to Picture Window
Books, Amy was an elementary art
teacher. She always impressed upon
her students that "everyone is an artist."
Amy lives in Mankato, Minnesota,
with her husband, Brad.

To Loren and Linda—thanks for always
directing me toward my talents.
To my Waconia students—every time you solve
a problem, you are thinking like an artist.
Be creative, and keep drawing!
ABM

Managing Editor: Bob Temple
Creative Director: Terri Foley
Editor: Sara E. Hoffmann
Editorial Adviser: Andrea Cascardi
Designer: Amy Bailey Muehlenhardt
Page production: Picture Window Books
The illustrations in this book were drawn with pencil.

Picture Window Books
5115 Excelsior Boulevard
Suite 232
Minneapolis, MN 55416
1-877-845-8392
www.picturewindowbooks.com

Printed in the United States of America.

Library of Congress Cataloging-in-Publication Data
Muehlenhardt, Amy Bailey, 1974-
Drawing and learning about dogs : using shapes and lines /
by Amy Bailey Muehlenhardt
p. cm — (Sketch it!)
Summary: Provides step-by-step instructions for drawing
different types of dogs, using circles, squares,
triangles, and other simple shapes.
Includes bibliographical references.
ISBN1-4048-0266-5 (Reinforced Library Binding)
1. Dogs in art—Juvenile literature.
2. Drawing—Technique—Juvenile literature. [1. Dogs in art.
2. Drawing—Technique.] I. Title.
NC783.8 D64 M84 2004
743.6'9772—dc22

2003018490

Table of Contents

Everyone Is an Artist

There is no right or wrong way to draw!

With a little patience and some practice, anyone can learn to draw. Did you know every picture begins as a simple shape? If you can draw shapes, you can draw anything.

The Basics of Drawing

line—a long mark made by a pen, a pencil, or another tool

guideline—a line used to help you draw. The guideline will be erased when your drawing is almost complete.

shade—to color in with your pencil

value—the lightness or darkness of an object

shape—the form or outline of an object or figure

diagonal—a shape or line that leans to the side

Before you begin, you will need:

a pencil
an eraser
lots of paper

Four Tips for Drawing

1. Draw very lightly.
To see how this is done, try drawing soft, medium, and dark lines. The softer you press, the lighter the lines will be.

2. Draw your shapes.
Connect them with a dark, sketchy line.

3. Add details.
Details are small things that make a good picture even better.

4. Smudge your art.
Use your finger to rub your lines. This will soften your picture and add shadows.

Let's get started!

Simple shapes help you draw.

Practice drawing these shapes before you begin:

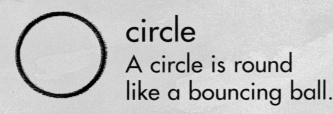 **circle**
A circle is round like a bouncing ball.

 **triangle**
A triangle has three sides and three corners.

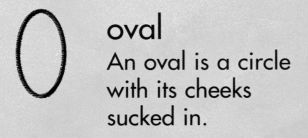 **oval**
An oval is a circle with its cheeks sucked in.

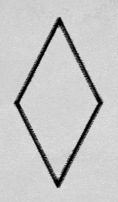 **diamond**
A diamond is two triangles put together.

arc
An arc is half of a circle. It looks like a turtle's shell.

square
A square has four equal sides and four corners.

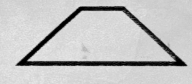 **trapezoid**
A trapezoid has four sides and four corners. Two of its sides are different lengths.

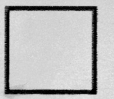 **crescent**
A crescent looks like a banana.

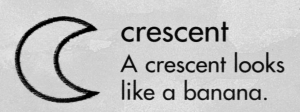  **rectangle**
A rectangle has two long sides, two short sides, and four corners.

You will also use lines when drawing.

Practice drawing these lines:

vertical
A vertical line stands tall like a tree.

zig zag

A zig-zag line is sharp and pointy.

horizontal
A horizontal line lies down and takes a nap.

wavy

A wavy line moves up and down like a roller coaster.

diagonal
A diagonal line leans to the side.

Remember to practice drawing.

While using this book, you may want to stop drawing at step five or six. That's great! Everyone is at a different drawing level.

dizzy
A dizzy line spins around and around.

Don't worry if your picture isn't perfect. The important thing is to have fun. You may wish to add details to your drawing. Is your dog on a leash? Is he chewing on a bone? Create a background.

Be creative!

Basset Hound

The basset hound is a medium-sized hunting dog. The hound has a keen nose for smelling things far away. Hounds have thick coats. They are great family dogs.

Step 1

Draw an oval for the head. Draw a smaller oval for the snout. This oval should overlap the first oval. Add two long ovals for the ears.

Step 2

Add a circle for the chest and an oval for the body.

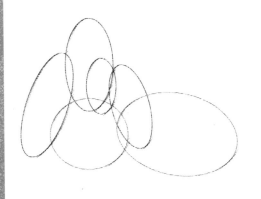

Step 3

Add two squares for the short front legs. Draw two ovals for the front paws.

Step 4

Draw a circle and an oval for a back leg. Add a crescent tail.

Step 5

Draw arcs for the eyes and a triangle for the nose. Connect the shapes with a darker, sketchy line.

Step 6

Using the side of your pencil, begin shading. Erase the lines you no longer need.

Step 7

Continue shading. Basset hounds have wavy lines under their eyes. Smudge the lines with your finger.

Miniature Schnauzer

The miniature schnauzer is full of life. The dog's coat is hard and wiry. It can be black, gray, or brown. A miniature schnauzer acts like a guard dog.

Step 1

Draw a circle for the head and a circle for the snout. Add two squares and two triangles for the ears.

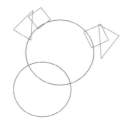

Step 2

Draw an oval for the body. The dog is sitting. Draw a little oval tail.

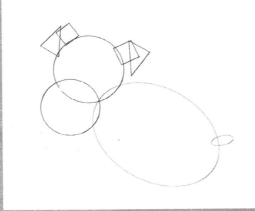

Step 3

Add two ovals below the face for front legs. Draw one circle for the back leg.

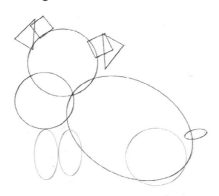

Step 4

Draw three ovals for the front and back paws. Draw two circle eyes. Add a square nose.

Step 5

Connect the shapes with a darker, sketchy line. Begin adding short lines for fur. Add a diagonal line for the mouth.

Step 6

Continue adding short, sketchy lines for fur. Erase the lines you no longer need.

Step 7

Fill in the entire dog with short lines for fur. Shade in the eyes and nose.

Bulldog

The bulldog came from England. It is a very courageous dog. A bulldog has a short and powerful jaw. The bulldog is known for being gentle and affectionate.

Step 1

Draw a rectangle for the body. Draw a circle for the head.

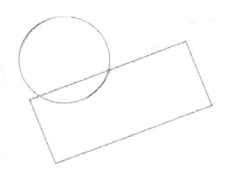

Step 2

Draw a smaller circle for the snout. Add two triangle ears.

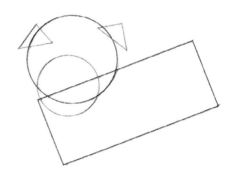

Step 3

Draw four rectangles for the legs and four squares for the feet.

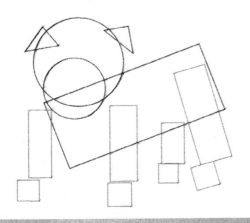

Step 4

Draw two arcs for the eyes. Add a triangle for the nose. Draw two crescents for the mouth and tail.

Step 5

Connect the shapes with a darker, sketchy line. Add curved lines for the sagging cheeks.

Step 6

Using the side of your pencil, begin shading. Erase the lines you no longer need.

Step 7

Continue shading. Make the eyes, nose, and mouth darker than the rest of the face.

Standard Poodle

Poodles come in three sizes: small, medium, and large. The largest poodles are called standard poodles. Standard poodles are friendly, intelligent dogs. They have coats that do not shed.

Step 1

Draw two circles for fur on the head and body. A poodle has fluffy fur.

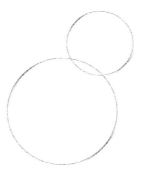

Step 2

Between the two circles, add a triangle. Draw two ovals for ears.

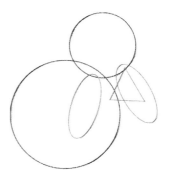

Step 3

Draw a rectangle for the body. Draw four rectangles for the front and back legs. Add a crescent tail.

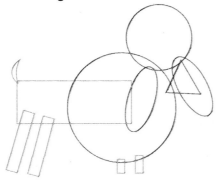

Step 4

Add small circles for balls of fur on the feet, tail, and back. Draw small squares for paws.

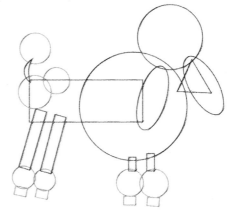

Step 5

Connect your shapes with a darker, sketchy line. Add small, dark ovals for the eye and nose.

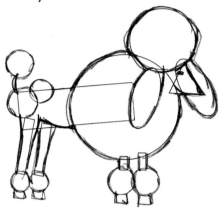

Step 6

Lightly shade in the fur. Draw curls in the balls of fur. Erase the lines you no longer need.

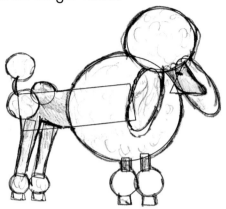

Step 7

Continue shading. Smudge the lines with your finger.

Golden Retriever

Golden retrievers are powerful and active. They are very friendly toward people and even other dogs. Golden retrievers are very intelligent. They love to run and play.

Step 1

Draw two circles for the head and snout. Add two ovals for ears.

Step 2

Draw an oval for the lower jaw. The oval should overlap the circle.

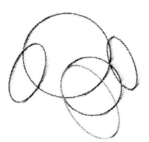

Step 3

Draw an oval for the tongue and an oval for the upper part of the body.

Step 4

Draw two ovals for eyes and an oval for the nose.

Step 5

Connect your shapes with a darker, sketchy line. Draw the nostrils with curved lines.

Step 6

Begin adding short, wavy lines for fur. Erase the lines you no longer need.

Step 7

Shade in with your pencil. Make the eyes, nose, and mouth darker than the rest of the face.

Dalmatian

Dalmatians are strong, active dogs. Dalmatians are white with black spots. They have short, smooth coats. Dalmatians are very outgoing.

Step 1

Draw a rectangle for the body and a square for the neck. Draw a circle for the head.

Step 2

Add a square for the snout. Draw two triangles for ears.

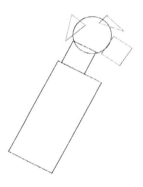

Step 3

Draw an oval for the back leg. Add two smaller ovals for the back paws.

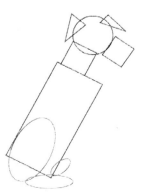

Step 4

Draw two long rectangles for the front legs. Add two squares for the front paws. Don't forget the crescent tail!

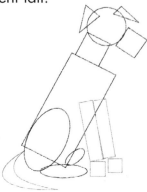

Step 5

Connect your shapes with a darker, sketchy line. Draw an arc for the eye and an oval for the nose.

Step 6

Draw circles and ovals for spots. Shade in each spot with your pencil. Erase the lines you no longer need.

Step 7

Continue shading in the spots. Darken the nose and eye.

Airedale Terrier

Airedale terriers have short, wiry coats. They were first used for hunting in England. The Airedale is known as the king of all sporting dogs.

Step 1

Draw a rectangle for the body. Draw a triangle for the neck. The triangle should overlap the rectangle.

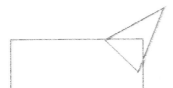

Step 2

Add a rectangle for the head. Draw a triangle for the eye and an arc for the nose.

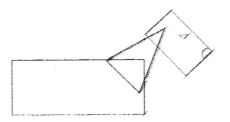

Step 3

Add four long rectangles for the legs.

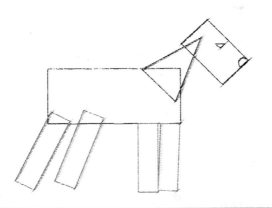

Step 4

Draw a crescent for the tail. Add two triangle ears.

Step 5

Connect your shapes with a darker, sketchy line.

Step 6

Add short, sketchy lines for fur. Erase the lines you no longer need.

Step 7

Continue adding short lines to shade in the Airedale. Darken the eye and nose. Add a curved line over the eye. Smudge the lines with your finger.

Chow Chow

Chow chows are powerful dogs used for hunting, protecting, and herding. Chow chows make wonderful family pets. They are very loyal.

Step 1

Draw a circle for the head. Draw a larger circle around the head for fur.

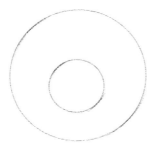

Step 2

Add two small circles for the eyes. Draw three arcs for the nose and ears.

Step 3

Add a circle and oval for the body. Draw an upside-down arc for the tail.

Step 4

Draw two ovals for the front legs and two rectangles for the back legs. Add four small rectangles for the paws.

Step 5

Connect your shapes with a darker, wavy line. Chow chows have a lot of fur. Shade in the eyes and nose.

Step 6

Use the side of your pencil to begin shading the fur. Erase the lines you no longer need.

Step 7

Continue shading in the fur. Shade in the eyes, nose, and mouth. Smudge the lines with your finger.

To Learn More

At the Library

Ames, Lee J. *Draw 50 Dogs*. Garden City, N.Y.: Doubleday, 1981.

Blackaby, Susan. *A Dog for You: Caring for Your Dog*. Minneapolis: Picture Window Books, 2003.

Emberley, Ed. *Ed Emberley's Drawing Book of Animals*. Boston: Little, Brown & Co., 1994.

Hart, Christopher. *Kids Draw Dogs, Puppies & Wolves*. New York: Watson-Guptill Publications, 2001.

Levin, Freddie. *1-2-3 Draw Pets and Farm Animals*. Columbus, N.C.: Peel Productions, 2000.

On the Web

Fact Hound

Fact Hound offers a safe, fun way to find Web sites related to this book. All of the sites on Fact Hound have been researched by our staff.

http://www.facthound.com

1. Visit the Fact Hound home page.
2. Enter a search word related to this book, or type in this special code: 1404802665.
3. Click on the FETCH IT button.

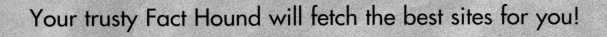

Your trusty Fact Hound will fetch the best sites for you!